Learning Log

A Learning Tool

Tony Nutley

Learning Log

By

Tony Nutley

Copyright © 2005 Tony Nutley

Published by Lulu.com

All Rights Reserved

First Edition

Cover design by Dhugal Dennison

www.ukcpd.net

Dedication

I would like to dedicate this publication to learners everywhere. I can honestly say that if you discover half of the joy I have from life long learning then you will be richer and happier then those that never open the box of wonder and personal discovery that is personal development and life long learning.

Big thanks to Dhugal for all his ongoing help with covers etc.

Huge thanks to Lee for his hard work proof reading and other suggestions.

Introduction

Keeping a learning log is one of the best tools to help you become an all-round learner. Your learning comes from experience as well as your studies because the Learning Log helps you articulate your learning and make it explicit.

In this workbook Tony Nutley provides all the encouragement, tools and techniques you will need to review, reflect and make conclusions and then plan to use your experiences - as well as helpful advice on how to continue benefiting from the results, after all you worked hard for this you may as well use your skills at every opportunity.

Life long learning or continuous personal development is the key element of personal success, both in our chosen field of work and especially in your personal lives. Our happiness and satisfaction in life comes from achieving goals, developing meaningful and lasting relationships, personal development will ALWAYS add to who you are.

Generally, those in life that are successful or happy are those that are always growing and are able to put what they learn into practice.

I wish you every success and personal happiness in whatever course of studies you have chosen to engage in.

Tony Nutley
Trainer & People Developer

Study Help

In order to keep a documentary record of what you are learning as you progress through your chosen course, it is strongly recommended that you keep a Learning Log. This idea has been used successfully in many universities and increasingly in NLP institutes. You will benefit as it requires you to organise, reflect and access your learning in a more conscious way.

Your Learning Log can be used to:

- Plan your study and make revisions as needed;
- Write down questions for your tutor as they arise;
- Make notes that will help you to carry out your study, e.g. on essay writing, preparing for examinations, previewing and reading texts in depth;
- Document your reading and viewing so that notes can be readily accessed for assignments and examinations;
- Document your reflections on your progress, problems encountered and ways that you might resolve them.

Useful Information on using a Learning Log

Over time you will develop your own ideas on using the log but the following points may help you initially:

- Always date each entry.
- Clearly distinguish entries about yourself and your life from information about your study.
- Keep your summaries and notes of readings and lectures separate from your opinions, comments and reflections on these.
- Use the section in your log to record questions to ask your tutor.
- Use the section for recording reading, viewings video etc and analysis.

Remember to make regular entries about:

- Books or articles you read that add to you knowledge.
- Your views on topics
- The websites you have found to be useful and why.
- Any helpful resources you find.
- New concepts that challenged your "map of the world".
- Glossary of new terms or jargon and examples of their use.

Using the log in this way will help you to reflect on all of the information presented by the tutor and to come to your own understanding of it. A Learning Log becomes a record of your entire journey in you chosen course of studies.

Identification Information

Student Name   _____

Course Name   _____

Tutor Name   _____

Start Date   _____

Finish Date   _____

Personal Statement Of Desired Outcomes From This Course

_____

_____

_____

_____

Personal Statement Of Evidence Of Success Criteria

_____

_____

_____

_____

Session / Seminar One

Content Title _____

Seminar Date _____

Personal Pre Study _____

Time Invested _____

Specifically What _____

Books _____

Web _____

Key Outcome _____

Important Because _____

_____

Resources Needed _____

Questions To Ask _____

_____

_____

_____

Post Seminar Analysis

Assess what you have achieved by answering the following questions.

What have I learnt from this session?

_____

_____

_____

What themes or patterns have I identified?

_____

_____

Were my questions answered?

_____

_____

_____

What did the tutor suggest I do between sessions?

_____

_____

What are the implications for my career from what I learnt?

_____

Post Seminar Reflections

Reflect on your learning and your experience of attending the session. What were your thoughts? What did you really enjoy? Was there anything you did not enjoy? How has this experience fitted with your goals, values and how you feel about learning this material?

_____

_____

_____

_____

_____

_____

_____

_____

_____

_____

Post Reflection Questions

What has come to mind? What questions do you have for next time? What additional study or activity will you do to prepare for the next session?

_____

_____

_____

_____

_____

_____

_____

_____

_____

_____

15

Session / Seminar Two

Content Title   _____

Seminar Date   _____

Personal Pre Study _____

Time Invested   _____

Specifically What   _____

Books   _____

Web   _____

Key Outcome   _____

Important Because _____

_____

Resources Needed _____

Questions To Ask   _____

_____

_____

_____

Post Seminar Analysis

Assess what you have achieved by answering the following questions.

What have I learnt from this session?

_____

_____

_____

What themes or patterns have I identified?

_____

_____

Were my questions answered?

_____

_____

_____

What did the tutor suggest I do between sessions?

_____

_____

What are the implications for my career from what I learnt?

_____

Post Seminar Reflections

Reflect on your learning and your experience of attending the session. What were your thoughts? What did you really enjoy? Was there anything you did not enjoy? How has this experience fitted with your goals, values and how you feel about learning this material?

_____

_____

_____

_____

_____

_____

_____

_____

_____

_____

_____

Post Reflection Questions

What has come to mind? What questions do you have for next time? What additional study or activity will you do to prepare for the next session?

_____

_____

_____

_____

_____

_____

_____

_____

_____

_____

Session / Seminar Three

Content Title   _____

Seminar Date   _____

Personal Pre Study   _____

Time Invested   _____

Specifically What   _____

Books   _____

Web   _____

Key Outcome   _____

Important Because   _____

                       _____

Resources Needed   _____

Questions To Ask   _____

                       _____

                       _____

                       _____

Post Seminar Analysis

Assess what you have achieved by answering the following questions.

What have I learnt from this session?

_____

_____

_____

What themes or patterns have I identified?

_____

_____

Were my questions answered?

_____

_____

_____

What did the tutor suggest I do between sessions?

_____

_____

What are the implications for my career from what I learnt?

_____

Post Seminar Reflections

Reflect on your learning and your experience of attending the session. What were your thoughts? What did you really enjoy? Was there anything you did not enjoy? How has this experience fitted with your goals, values and how you feel about learning this material?

_____

_____

_____

_____

_____

_____

_____

_____

_____

_____

Post Reflection Questions

What has come to mind? What questions do you have for next time? What additional study or activity will you do to prepare for the next session?

_____

_____

_____

_____

_____

_____

_____

_____

_____

_____

Session / Seminar Four

Content Title   _____

Seminar Date   _____

Personal Pre Study _____

Time Invested   _____

Specifically What   _____

Books   _____

Web   _____

Key Outcome   _____

Important Because   _____

_____

Resources Needed   _____

Questions To Ask   _____

_____

_____

_____

Post Seminar Analysis

Assess what you have achieved by answering the following questions.

What have I learnt from this session?

_____

_____

_____

What themes or patterns have I identified?

_____

_____

Were my questions answered?

_____

_____

_____

What did the tutor suggest I do between sessions?

_____

_____

What are the implications for my career from what I learnt?

_____

Post Seminar Reflections

Reflect on your learning and your experience of attending the session. What were your thoughts? What did you really enjoy? Was there anything you did not enjoy? How has this experience fitted with your goals, values and how you feel about learning this material?

_____

_____

_____

_____

_____

_____

_____

_____

_____

_____

Post Reflection Questions

What has come to mind? What questions do you have for next time? What additional study or activity will you do to prepare for the next session?

_____

_____

_____

_____

_____

_____

_____

_____

_____

_____

Session / Seminar Five

Content Title   _____

Seminar Date   _____

Personal Pre Study   _____

Time Invested   _____

Specifically What   _____

Books   _____

Web   _____

Key Outcome   _____

Important Because   _____

                       _____

Resources Needed   _____

Questions To Ask   _____

                       _____

                       _____

                       _____

Post Seminar Analysis

Assess what you have achieved by answering the following questions.

What have I learnt from this session?

_____

_____

_____

What themes or patterns have I identified?

_____

_____

Were my questions answered?

_____

_____

_____

What did the tutor suggest I do between sessions?

_____

_____

What are the implications for my career from what I learnt?

_____

Post Seminar Reflections

Reflect on your learning and your experience of attending the session. What were your thoughts? What did you really enjoy? Was there anything you did not enjoy? How has this experience fitted with your goals, values and how you feel about learning this material?

_____

_____

_____

_____

_____

_____

_____

_____

_____

_____

Post Reflection Questions

What has come to mind? What questions do you have for next time? What additional study or activity will you do to prepare for the next session?

_____

_____

_____

_____

_____

_____

_____

_____

_____

_____

_____

Session / Seminar Six

Content Title   _____

Seminar Date   _____

Personal Pre Study   _____

Time Invested   _____

Specifically What   _____

Books   _____

Web   _____

Key Outcome   _____

Important Because   _____

_____

Resources Needed   _____

Questions To Ask   _____

_____

_____

_____

Post Seminar Analysis

Assess what you have achieved by answering the following questions.

What have I learnt from this session?

_____

_____

_____

What themes or patterns have I identified?

_____

_____

Were my questions answered?

_____

_____

_____

What did the tutor suggest I do between sessions?

_____

_____

What are the implications for my career from what I learnt?

_____

Post Seminar Reflections

Reflect on your learning and your experience of attending the session. What were your thoughts? What did you really enjoy? Was there anything you did not enjoy? How has this experience fitted with your goals, values and how you feel about learning this material?

_____

_____

_____

_____

_____

_____

_____

_____

_____

_____

Post Reflection Questions

What has come to mind? What questions do you have for next time? What additional study or activity will you do to prepare for the next session?

_____

_____

_____

_____

_____

_____

_____

_____

_____

_____

_____

Session / Seminar Seven

Content Title   _____

Seminar Date   _____

Personal Pre Study   _____

Time Invested   _____

Specifically What   _____

Books   _____

Web   _____

Key Outcome   _____

Important Because   _____

                        _____

Resources Needed   _____

Questions To Ask   _____

                        _____

                        _____

                        _____

Post Seminar Analysis

Assess what you have achieved by answering the following questions.

What have I learnt from this session?

_____

_____

_____

What themes or patterns have I identified?

_____

_____

Were my questions answered?

_____

_____

_____

What did the tutor suggest I do between sessions?

_____

_____

What are the implications for my career from what I learnt?

_____

Post Seminar Reflections

Reflect on your learning and your experience of attending the session. What were your thoughts? What did you really enjoy? Was there anything you did not enjoy? How has this experience fitted with your goals, values and how you feel about learning this material?

_____

_____

_____

_____

_____

_____

_____

_____

_____

_____

Post Reflection Questions

What has come to mind? What questions do you have for next time? What additional study or activity will you do to prepare for the next session?

_____

_____

_____

_____

_____

_____

_____

_____

_____

_____

_____

Session / Seminar Eight

Content Title   _____

Seminar Date   _____

Personal Pre Study _____

Time Invested   _____

Specifically What   _____

Books   _____

Web   _____

Key Outcome   _____

Important Because   _____

_____

Resources Needed   _____

Questions To Ask   _____

_____

_____

_____

Post Seminar Analysis

Assess what you have achieved by answering the following questions.

What have I learnt from this session?

_____

_____

_____

What themes or patterns have I identified?

_____

_____

Were my questions answered?

_____

_____

_____

What did the tutor suggest I do between sessions?

_____

_____

What are the implications for my career from what I learnt?

_____

Post Seminar Reflections

Reflect on your learning and your experience of attending the session. What were your thoughts? What did you really enjoy? Was there anything you did not enjoy? How has this experience fitted with your goals, values and how you feel about learning this material?

_____

_____

_____

_____

_____

_____

_____

_____

_____

_____

Post Reflection Questions

What has come to mind? What questions do you have for next time? What additional study or activity will you do to prepare for the next session?

_____

_____

_____

_____

_____

_____

_____

_____

_____

_____

Session / Seminar Nine

Content Title _____

Seminar Date _____

Personal Pre Study _____

Time Invested _____

Specifically What _____

Books _____

Web _____

Key Outcome _____

Important Because _____

_____

Resources Needed _____

Questions To Ask _____

_____

_____

_____

Post Seminar Analysis

Assess what you have achieved by answering the following questions.

What have I learnt from this session?

_____

_____

_____

What themes or patterns have I identified?

_____

_____

Were my questions answered?

_____

_____

_____

What did the tutor suggest I do between sessions?

_____

_____

What are the implications for my career from what I learnt?

_____

Post Seminar Reflections

Reflect on your learning and your experience of attending the session. What were your thoughts? What did you really enjoy? Was there anything you did not enjoy? How has this experience fitted with your goals, values and how you feel about learning this material?

_____

_____

_____

_____

_____

_____

_____

_____

_____

_____

Post Reflection Questions

What has come to mind? What questions do you have for next time? What additional study or activity will you do to prepare for the next session?

_____

_____

_____

_____

_____

_____

_____

_____

_____

_____

_____

Session / Seminar Nine

Content Title   _____

Seminar Date   _____

Personal Pre Study _____

Time Invested   _____

Specifically What   _____

Books   _____

Web   _____

Key Outcome   _____

Important Because   _____

_____

Resources Needed _____

Questions To Ask   _____

_____

_____

_____

Post Seminar Analysis

Assess what you have achieved by answering the following questions.

What have I learnt from this session?

_____

_____

_____

What themes or patterns have I identified?

_____

_____

Were my questions answered?

_____

_____

_____

What did the tutor suggest I do between sessions?

_____

_____

What are the implications for my career from what I learnt?

_____

Post Seminar Reflections

Reflect on your learning and your experience of attending the session. What were your thoughts? What did you really enjoy? Was there anything you did not enjoy? How has this experience fitted with your goals, values and how you feel about learning this material?

_____

_____

_____

_____

_____

_____

_____

_____

_____

_____

Post Reflection Questions

What has come to mind? What questions do you have for next time? What additional study or activity will you do to prepare for the next session?

_____

_____

_____

_____

_____

_____

_____

_____

_____

_____

Session / Seminar Ten

Content Title _____

Seminar Date _____

Personal Pre Study _____

Time Invested _____

Specifically What _____

Books _____

Web _____

Key Outcome _____

Important Because _____

_____

Resources Needed _____

Questions To Ask _____

_____

_____

_____

Post Seminar Analysis

Assess what you have achieved by answering the following questions.

What have I learnt from this session?

_____

_____

_____

What themes or patterns have I identified?

_____

_____

Were my questions answered?

_____

_____

_____

What did the tutor suggest I do between sessions?

_____

_____

What are the implications for my career from what I learnt?

_____

Post Seminar Reflections

Reflect on your learning and your experience of attending the session. What were your thoughts? What did you really enjoy? Was there anything you did not enjoy? How has this experience fitted with your goals, values and how you feel about learning this material?

_____

_____

_____

_____

_____

_____

_____

_____

_____

_____

<u>Post Reflection Questions</u>

What has come to mind? What questions do you have for next time? What additional study or activity will you do to prepare for the next session?

_____

_____

_____

_____

_____

_____

_____

_____

_____

_____

_____

Post Seminar Reflections & Outcome Analysis

Reflect and analyse your journey and discover what you have achieved.

Have your initial outcomes been met?

_____

How do you know this, what evidence can you point to?

_____

What have you enjoyed?

_____

What was a challenge?

_____

How are you different?

_____

What practical skills have you at your disposal now that you did not have at the beginning of your course?

_____

What has been the biggest learning?

_____

Would you recommend this course of studies?

_____

Can you explain why?

_____

What is the next step in your personal development?

_____

Final Essay

Based on what you have recorded on in this learning log, write a short essay (1000 words) on your journey, what you have achieved and give specific examples of how you have been using your knowledge, skills and new behaviours.

Essay Notes

_____

_____

_____

_____

_____

Visit us at

www.ukcpd.net

We run several courses and offer various personal development and coaching programs.

Sign up for the regular e-zine

I wish you ongoing success and happiness

Tony Nutley
Trainer & Life Coach

The UK College of Personal Development
Suite 180 116 Commercial Road
Swindon Wilts SN1 5BD

Printed in the United Kingdom
by Lightning Source UK Ltd.
134289UK00001B/1-6/A

9 781411 663138